Relationship Sanity

Cut the Crap That Makes Relationships Fail

Jason J. Andrew, MA, LPC-S

NEWMAN SPRINGS PUBLISHING
320 Broad Street
Red Bank, NJ 07701

First originally published by Newman Springs Publishing 2022

ISBN 978-1-68498-645-3 (Paperback)
ISBN 978-1-68498-648-4 (Digital)

Printed in the United States of America

To Chloe, Lilly, and Jace

Contents

So You Say You Want
to Get Married?

How do you define marriage? Is there a stigma about marriage? What are fake relationships? What is the real reason people get together? It seems that when a person grows up and observes their role models in relationships, that modeling appears to be the _parents_ first influence on the person about how they define marriage. This person grows up and may experience different models of marriage. The differences appear strange at first, but as time goes on, they may begin to adapt to a different way of thinking. Let's say we have a person who grows up with parents who stay together for their kids yet remain unhappy and may appear distant from each other, thus showing an unhealthy model of marriage. There is a lot of research about what is the best model when a married couple has an epiphany that they are not healthy together. What if this child talks with a friend of theirs and that friend says, "My parents sleep in separate bedrooms." Does this child think that's odd because their parents sleep in the same bed? What gets me thinking at night are the following questions: Why do people choose to be married? For financial reasons, pride reasons, or other unhealthy and selfish reasons? Or do people get married because they think being married will solve _dont_ personal problems, like loneliness or codependency? Why do people _want_ wear wedding rings? Is it to show off to other people, or is it a true _this_ symbol that person is committed to the relationship? What I wonder is, Can people be married yet be fully individual and not need another person to satisfy all their needs? I wanted to write a book to help people considering the marriage relationship really understand why they are getting married and also think about the bigger picture about being married. In other words, what is the purpose of this

Manifestation

marriage for each person? It is my hope that this book would help somebody be more prepared when considering marriage.

Considering divorce?

I looked it up. The song is "Breakfast at Tiffany's." Read these lyrics and ask yourself what you have left in common with your ex-partner.

Breakfast at Tiffany's

Deep Blue Something

You'll say, we've got nothing in common
No common ground to start from
And we're falling apart
You'll say, the world has come between us
Our lives have come between us
Still I know you just don't care
And I said what about Breakfast at Tiffany's
She said I think I remember the film
And as I recall I think we both kind of liked it
And I said well that's the one thing we've got
I see you the only one who knew me
And now your eyes see through me
I guess I was wrong
So what now
It's plain to see we're over
And I hate when things are over
When so much is left undone
And I said what about Breakfast at Tiffany's
She said I think I remember the film
And as I recall I think we both kind of liked it
And I said well that's the one thing we've got
You'll say, that we've got nothing in common
No common ground to start from
And we're falling apart
You'll say the world has come between us
Our lives have come between us

Still I know you just don't care
And, as I recall, I think, we both kind of liked it,
And I said, "Well that's, the one thing we got."

Songwriters: Pipes Todd David
For noncommercial use only
Data from: Musixmatch

↗ breeakups

How do you make a decision about divorce? The big picture about marriage needs to be understood. When considering divorce, you have to understand all the costs that apply. For example, you have the cost of a lawyer. You need to have lawyers help you separate assets. I think people don't understand how much money it takes to get a divorce. You also have the emotional toll on the children.

Back to why people get married. Some people may get married to only fulfill their own sexual needs—in other words, selfish reasons. It could be to satisfy each person's sexual needs, a possibly healthier model.

I just wish more people would get married for healthy reasons and not rush into marriage after a disappointing life event.

I have learned that sexual activities in the 1960s were more open than today. It makes me wonder if marriage in the twenty-first century is more messed up than it was in the twentieth century or if it has always been messed up.

Open marriages will allow for a couple to be married yet see other sexual partners. There are also swingers. Many different marriage ideas are out there in this twenty-first century.

Influenced by no one? Can an adult be able to take care of themselves without the help or influence of others? Unless you are a child abandoned by your parents and who gets raised by wolves, you would understand that everyone is influenced by some being or even some environment. I recently learned about attachment theory, which explains how people's influences as a child can explain a reason *dad* they act and think the way they do as adults. I think if someone wants *&* to get married, they should learn if they have attachment issues and *mom* learn if they need to make any adjustments before getting married.

└yes

I believe that as of February 20, 2020, I realized how I lost myself in my marriage. I did not develop a healthy sense of me. When my youngest turned nine, I lost purpose. I am learning a healthier way of living. I would not have thought I'd be writing about divorce. If at least one person out there learns to really make sure they don't rush into a relationship, I have fulfilled my purpose of writing this book.

I feel like the music industry profits from bad relationships. A lot of artists write songs about breakups, separation, and even divorce.

I wonder where those people who get divorced get support from. There are many support groups that focus on hope. Who focuses on reality?

I don't look forward to dating again.

I recently met a millennial who explained to me that they did not want to be married because they didn't see the purpose of getting married. It seems like our American culture is shifting to a new model of long-term relationships. I also met a coworker who told me that she did not see the purpose of getting married when the perks were the same. Perks would be referring to everything except having been married.

I recently observed relationships where couples who met in high school appear to stay together. Also, I observed that couples who are from the same geographic area also appear to stay together. What I wonder about my relationship is how my spouse and I came from very different geographic areas, and it may be important to evaluate before marriage if two people from different places can be married.

My wife suggested her opinion of how to move toward divorce. She shared her opinion. She stated, "We live in the same house. We don't talk about our relationship. We only talk about how to take care of the kids and the bills." Our house felt like a war zone with negativity flowing throughout and people yelling at each other and nobody spending time together. It felt like a hotel where everyone comes home and just goes into their rooms and plays on their devices and eats in their rooms. My wife would say, "All I know is that the current plan is to coexist together and take care of our kids, house chores, and bills." I have recently had my eyes opened to a new understanding that our relationship was unhealthy and screwed up. The hardest part of living in a place where there is a lack of love and support for each other is trying to act like things are normal when it is obvious even to a stranger who happens to visit the house that things in this household are very negative. So you might be asking, "What is the purpose of that short story?" My purpose would be to understand that when two people want a divorce and there are kids involved, there is no right answer on how to manage a household. Yet there needs to be a plan on how to talk about the divorce even if it's hard to talk about. My experience is that my wife never wanted to talk about things and that made it hard to know what the plan was. Now if you would ask my wife, she would say, "I already told you. There is no new news. We are coexisting," and it's difficult when one person feels lost.

Is There Individual Hope?

1. We are not promised tomorrow. This is a new way of living. I find myself trying to enjoy every day to the fullest! On the days I work, I attempt to do something enjoyable or different in the evenings. I used to just work, then come home, and just do routine activities. Now I realize how important it is to enjoy things minute by minute.

2. Mindfulness is another way to explain this idea. There are twenty-four hours in a day. You sleep for eight hours and work for eight hours. That leaves eight hours to do something that is enjoyable. That is one-third of your day that I am learning needs to be used for something enjoyable. The year is 2020, and I really don't recall setting a new year's resolution. Yet now it is the first week of March, and I am realizing that I have a resolution that involves doing something enjoyable every day of my life going forward. Done are the days when I just kept doing the daily routine because it led to feelings of sadness and anger. And even on a budget, there are fun things that can be done. I think the biggest change I have made is realizing that life is short and to enjoy life to the fullest. My mom bought me a coffee mug that says, "Life is a gift. Enjoy every moment." Don't let other people tell you what you should do. It is important to be true to yourself. A wise man once said, "Stop doing stupid shit," which I interpret as "Stop doing things that don't feed you."

3. Consult others. It is important to first ask yourself what you want. There are plenty of strategies to help you decide what you want. It is my observation that most people ask friends, family, or coworkers for their opinion. Opinions

doesn't matter who they are!

can be helpful yet also very unhealthy at times. My experience is the only thing I can speak about. Everyone's experience is different. I find everyone wants to tell you what they think you should do. Some people can't wait to jump in and save the day. Others sit back and just watch to see what happens. I think the reason we go asking for help is to feel supported. Human beings are relational and need others beside them during a divorce. People can find themselves going to their doctor and getting prescribed sleep aids due to the stress making them unable to fall asleep at night. Some people find themselves using substances to numb the pain. Some may become addicted to various things that make them numb the feelings. *vaping*

Kids are more aware than you realize about the environment. My oldest knew more than I realized. The younger two would make references that made me realize they knew something bad was going on.

Is There a Science to the Reaction to Divorce?

a break up (handwritten)

Mental health issues are very common reactions to divorce. Many people can experience symptoms of depression, anxiety, thoughts of suicide, and even thoughts of homicide. As a professional counselor, I understand how these symptoms are common in divorce. Yet I was recently challenged in this thinking. A person who has these types of symptoms can be identified as selfish. If you or someone you know is going through a divorce and they identify as having these types of symptoms, of course it is important to validate these symptoms/feelings. Yet I would encourage everyone to not let these symptoms consume them. It's so important to begin to do things like hobbies, exercise, or anything that may keep you engaged socially with others. Maybe play games with your kids. Maybe think of new activities you have never done before. The time after divorce, I think, is the most complicated time for a person to go through. It is very important to find yourself, reevaluate your priorities, and begin to learn how to be happy alone. I have met a number of people who have gone through divorce, and they always stress the importance of learning how to be happy alone first, especially when you want to have that rebound relationship. All I know is that I found it very important to make new friends in settings that I had never considered before. I am meeting and becoming friends with a number of people whom I would have never considered meeting and having social interaction with. I find it helpful to have more than one new group of friends. This way, when you have something come up, you will have a number of different people to choose from for helping with things.

I lost myself and need to find myself again. I find myself learning how to set a budget again and how to manage my schedule.

Sexual Identity

what is sexual identity

I think it is important to be true to yourself. I have read some books recently that made me think how important it is for all people to evaluate their sexual identity. I think a lot of people do not evaluate this when they get married, and thus, getting divorced will force that person to reevaluate their sexual identity.

Coronavirus in 2020 forced many people to practice social distancing. One observation is it has forced people to use technology to continue to have social interactions. Another observation is more people are walking, and I experienced social interaction with people saying hi or waving hi. I have observed people expressing their needs, both sexually and socially, on social media.

Epiphany!

At 2:45 p.m. on April 13, 2020, I had an epiphany. I need to learn that I cannot run away from my problems anymore. I have lived half of my life running away from those who have hurt me. Now I am learning how to live in the same house, sit in my feelings, and stop acting depressed because of negative feelings around me. I have to sit up straight; keep my head up, shoulders back; and look confident. I call this Jason 2.0.

Lauryn 2.0

Children

When you have kids and get divorced, it is important to know they need to be a priority. Keeping communication open is very important. My kids were all teenagers, and most teenagers would rather do things with their friends, and that was my experience. I want people to know that when you get divorced and you have kids, they need to be a priority in your life and you need to make an effort to do activities that they like to do. When divorcing, one can think it's time to be selfish. That can be, but it is important to find a good balance between being selfish and being available to your kids.

selfish & family

Finances

I personally struggle with managing finances. I definitely have more knowledge at my current age than I did when I was in my early twenties. I find it helps to talk with friends who are trained in financial management and learn to trust yourself and have confidence you can find a way to manage your money after a divorce. I have many friends these days who will give advice, which is fine. I also am learning to trust myself. I find worry is also something I don't want to rule my being. There are classes you can take to teach you how to manage your finances. Public schools have yet to have this class that is very much needed more than ever.

.

Lesson Learned

I learned this at a recent counseling appointment. The reason I asked others for help is because as a child, I was trained to not think for myself. I was a good student who was trained as a child to not think for myself and to ask others for direction in life. I have learned how unhealthy this is.

I want this book to teach my kids and everyone who reads it to identify who you are and what groups in this world you want to associate with and to ultimately think for yourself and not allow any person to tell you what to do with your life. Also, live your life the way you want to live it. Enjoy every day of your life. Experiment, try things that you may not do, and be open to lifestyles. If anything is learned, it is important to be true to yourself. Don't let anybody influence you in a way that is not true to yourself. Sometimes we are not sure who shaped our life in certain ways. All that matters is taking the step to say, "Today, I will do things differently." If everyone would live their own lives true to themselves, I think we could have a better society.

Dreams

I am learning how it is very common to have dreams about the relationship you are divorcing from. One morning I awoke feeling like I just had a difficult discussion with my ex.

At 12:30 a.m. my oldest child woke me up, saying, "Dad, I heard an alarm going off." I said I would walk the house. The house was clear, but my ex-wife's room light was on, and the door was locked.

The next thing that I knew was my attempt to pick the lock and see if she was okay. We ended up in an argument.

I was so pissed off because all I was doing was checking to make sure she was okay.

She said I invaded her privacy. She then proceeded to say she would kill me if I ever invaded her privacy again.

I learned from this experience that my story only makes sense to me and her story only makes sense to her.

We were able to talk through the situation with professional help.

I was just so pissed at her reaction.

Does Time Heal?

I found myself, this past calendar week, feeling happier than I had in months. I asked myself why. There are a number of reasons. If I found myself happier, was it because I had turned a corner in regard to accepting my divorce? Did I find myself happier because I was just choosing to be happier? Was I happier because I had started meeting other women on dating apps? Was I happier because my mindset had fully accepted that life goes on past divorce? It seems very interesting to me that I was even getting along better with my ex during this past week. I know that people will say, "Time heals all wounds." I will say that I am learning that it is true that time does heal wounds. I also will say that I am learning that meeting new friends, male and female, is very important for me right now. When I meet new people, it makes me feel like I am helping my need to feel connected at a time like this. In 2020, I did join a club that years ago I would have never considered joining and that I have really enjoyed connecting with. Word of advice: If you are divorcing, you need to research and even talk with people about clubs and gatherings near you that you can join, even if you find yourself thinking, *I'd never try that*. You should actually sign up now! You also need to be willing to go to social gatherings. I recently connected with a person and found myself days later being invited to a small evening gathering.

When I arrived, the host said, "Man, you are brave to come into a place where most don't know you!"

I said, "Hey, I am trying some new things, and I am just happy I was invited and glad to participate in a relaxing and fun evening!"

This evening was very enjoyable. I made new friends, enjoyed the conversations, and even had some great drinks. A couple days later, I ran into a person I met that night, and it felt good to have someone remember me.

Pandemic

During a time when this virus shut down many businesses and restaurants, it was a challenge to connect with people. Zoom video chat became very popular. I did try a Zoom video chat with two different groups I was involved in, and it was good. I definitely can say it was a great way to connect with people. I did recently ask someone if they preferred video connections or physical connections. They said physical connections. I know for me I want the face-to-face physical contact with another person. I believe we are meant for face-to-face physical contact.

Bored?

After divorce, I find myself staying busy by writing my book, watching television shows, and talking on the phone. I also try to spend time with my kids at home. My youngest likes to play chess with me. I am not a pro at the game. I just recently learned how to play when I worked as a counselor at a nonprofit counseling center where the kids had chess teams and taught me how to play. I also recently was talking with a friend who said I need to continue to look for more activities. I spent a weekend away from my kids once. I had called and tried to set up some meal dates. I did enjoy the time to myself, as most parents would gladly take, yet I also felt a short period of boredom. I believe there is nothing wrong with boredom. Just don't let boredom overtake your being. Nothing good ever comes out of allowing boredom to overtake your being. It can be very tempting to do unhealthy things. If you find yourself saying, "Man, I'm bored," just allow yourself to regroup and find something to pass the time. It is important to know how you are not alone. There are people out there who are experiencing the same feelings you feel, who are having the same thoughts you are having. One good friend recently said a very brief statement that makes sense while recovering from divorce. Keep your head up! I think that is a great statement, because for me I used to look depressed, which meant my head was always down. I am just learning so much about myself, learning that we are not promised tomorrow, learning *you only live once* (YOLO)! Even as a professional counselor, I find myself learning new ways to help people based on my new experiences during divorce. I wanted this book to be helpful to many people. Our society has so many different types of people, and it is my hope that something I wrote in this book really can help them.

Religion?

I will keep this brief. I know the importance of faith in people's lives, and faith has been a helpful support idea for many. I also think people need to be more open to other beliefs and not give a shit what friends and family think. Everyone is different, and as long as people are true to themselves, that is all that matters to me! Be honest with yourself about your religious beliefs and faith.

Christianity

✯ Be Honest with Yourself about Everything!

Very important

If you are not honest with yourself, change now! Do one thing differently next time, and overtime you should find yourself making better choices, and I would even hope for a better mood and better thought patterns!

What is wrong with that? Who doesn't want to have a better lifestyle and feel better overall? I know I do, and I have begun to see the benefits of making changes like this. I will also say that it helps to have encouraging friends as well as people who can speak the truth to you, even if it hurts! *jaz & donna*

Stages of Divorce

Today I thought about how getting divorced has stages. Back in January to February, I found myself separated and going out to bars and hanging out with friends more just to get away from my ex. In March, my ex filed the petition for divorce, as well as writing the decree. The COVID-19 pandemic affected our lives in March and April. During these times, I tried to do virtual meetings with friends and even social distanced by going to a friend's office and just sitting six feet apart and socializing. Now in May I find myself beginning to consider meeting new friends. I even feel a sense that everyone who divorces must find time to develop their true selves. I recently have felt a couple moments of feeling bored, yet I was also able to find something to do to pass the time, focusing on listening to comedians or watching a comedy show like *SNL* or even trying to find a new book to read or a new show to binge-watch on Netflix. I will admit how difficult it is to co-parent with my ex while living together during this pandemic. I look forward to having my own place next month. I have been reading books more, which I am glad about because I used to hate to read. I've had two new friends share good books to read and have enjoyed that new hobby. Another hobby is writing this book on relationships. I do believe I am finding my true self again. I recently facetimed my parents, and they said I looked good. They were saying that to encourage me, because of what I am going through. I have been texting friends more than usual. I continue to be social, just in different and unique ways. Another challenging situation for me is talking with the in-laws. I do find myself looking at Facebook more than usual, another way to be connected socially.

I do wonder if this book will make sense. I find myself randomly writing and wondering if in the future it will develop into a helpful book about relationships. I hope this book gets finished in 2020.

I guess I should say that when it comes to this sixty-day waiting period for divorce, I really have a hard time with the waiting, but I am still living with the ex and kids while I wait for my apartment.

Live day by day. You only live once. I will try anything at least once. We are not promised tomorrow. These are four mantras I am trying to live by. I am even trying to be true to myself for a change. I have been walking daily, which helps in many ways. The idea I would suggest when divorcing is to find what brings you joy and do it as much as you can during this time. It can only help.

◁ Don't expect a life where you wait for other people to care about you! *will*
   Live a life where you are comfortable thinking for yourself and making the tough calls.

need to work on this

Online Dating?

You want to date again? Good luck!

In the year 2020, a pandemic happened and drove an increase in online dating. I found myself talking with a friend who made a comment that online dating could lead to a new relationship. I signed up for a couple dating apps.

"You just got divorced!" This was a statement I heard a lot!

Who's in charge of this dating thing? This was my internal dialogue when I heard that observation from others.

My opinion only: Evaluate when you are ready to date again. Don't let people you date influence your decision. You are in charge of yourself, not them.

Don't Be a Pussy

Remember that if you get married, never become a pussy! My observation is that some men don't stand up for themselves. Another observation is men might please their spouse too much. Don't be a guy who gets married and over the years becomes more of a pussy because you just do whatever your spouse wants to do and you lose your individual identity and individual goals in life. One day I met a guy who just read me and said, "Man, you are pathetic. You need to stop being a pussy." He was right! I was so blind to my own identity that I had no idea I was acting this way, and I am grateful for this man who identified this part of my life that was not healthy. Maybe you are reading this book and saying, "OMG! That's me!" Start today to evaluate what you can change to stop being a pussy. *begging for will back when he mistreated me*

Those who have been pussies for too long go to a bar or restaurant by themselves and talk with whoever is there and share their pussy story with a stranger and just see what advice they share with them. It can be enlightening, or it might even make you feel more depressed. Yet you can only come up from this low point! There is a brighter future ahead of you. *I belive this*

Maybe you enjoy being a pussy. More power to ya! My opinion only: My life became so much better after I stopped being a pussy! I have kids, and I did not want to teach them by example how to be a pussy. I'd rather teach them how to grow up confident, self-sufficient, and fully happy with their life!

being a pussy was me being afraid to leave will and move on

or seeing him move on

Stop Saying, "I Don't Know"

If you find yourself saying this phrase, you need to begin saying, "I know what I want!" Saying "I don't know" is a statement that you have lost the ability to think for yourself. We all need to think for ourselves. I know some people have a story from their past that they use to say why it's hard to think for themselves. I am not discounting those stories, yet these past stories don't have to still apply, and people can learn how to think for themselves. Basic brainstorming is a good place to begin.

"idk if I ever want to be in a relationship with will again"

An Increase in Drama after Divorce

Be warned that if you decide to divorce, there is usually an increase in drama after a divorce. I did not expect this increase of drama. It came from many angles. I thought that when my divorce was finalized, all drama would end. That is not what happened, and when I asked others who were divorced, they said the same thing. People would share with me that sometimes the drama lasted years. Others said it wasn't as long. I just want people to know the possibility of an increase in drama after a divorce.

The more you are prepared, the better you can cope with this stage of a relationship.

stay away from drama

We All Need to Learn to Support Ourselves!

So many people end up in financial problems after divorce. Many of these problems would be avoided if we all knew how to support ourselves! Financial stress is common in divorce.

Debt

After four months of divorce, debt haunted my mind. Most couples who divorce will accrue some form of debt after the divorce. I am not a financial person, so please know my thoughts are from experience. I found myself racking up charges on a new credit card, and I have heard this happens a lot with people who divorce. Maybe they need to go out and live it up or go on vacations they never got to go on or even just want to buy things they never got to buy when they were married. The lesson here is to be smart about accruing more debt than you already have. I know when I divorced, I had debt from when I took out a loan from my 401K. I also had college debt, debt from car repairs and new furniture, and even debt from a ring I bought my ex-wife before we divorced. It is probably best at this point in the book to say that if you are in a lot of debt, there are plenty of resources out there to help. The internet would be your assistant.

✴ Saying Goodbye to Unhealthy People

A wise man once told me friends come and go in our life. That wise man was my father. After divorcing, I chose to say goodbye to a person I met at the end of my divorce. This person was associated with my ex-wife, as a lot of my friends were since I wasn't from this area and she was. My opinion only: I think that it is healthy to purge unhealthy relationships after a divorce. My purpose in saying goodbye to one friend was to separate myself from anyone who knew my ex-wife first. I wanted to find and develop my own friends this time. I think we all need to evaluate how healthy our relationships are and consider if we need to keep or purge those relationships. Guys, make sure you have your own group of friends before you get married. Losing your own friends is unhealthy. And don't let your spouse force you to become friends with all her friends. I believe two people need to have their own lives and their own friends. And just maybe the spouse will become friends with your friends and vice versa.

Don't Lose Yourself in a Marriage!

(handwritten: Relationship above "Marriage")

It is so important to develop your identity. I lost my identity in my marriage. I thought that it was my job as a husband to just do everything my wife wanted to do. I understand now this was modeled to me as a child. I also understand after my divorce that I was not myself at the end of that relationship. It makes sense now that I wasn't doing activities that I wanted to do. I was not speaking up to my wife about my needs, which was totally my fault. *(handwritten: dating Will)*

According to Google, comedian Jeff Allen believes that he invented the phrase *happy wife, happy life*. I really believed this when I was married. I don't anymore! Men, you need to stand up, be empowered to do what you want to do, and find a wife who loves you for who you are. I guess you could lose yourself and be okay with that lifestyle. I have known people who do and are happy. It is a choice, and you have to accept the consequences of that choice.

Love, Love, Love...

I looked it up on my Amazon Music app and looked at the lyrics of the Beatles song "All You Need Is Love." Read these lyrics and come up with your opinion:

Love, love, love
Love, love, love
Love, love, love
There's nothing you can do that can't be done
Nothing you can sing that can't be sung
Nothing you can say, but you can learn how to play
*   the game*
It's easy
Nothing you can make that can't be made
No one you can save that can't be saved
Nothing you can do, but you can learn how to be
*   you in time*
It's easy
All you need is love
All you need is love
All you need is love, love
Love is all you need
All you need is love
All you need is love
All you need is love, love
Love is all you need
There's nothing you can know that isn't known
Nothing you can see that isn't shown
There's nowhere you can be that isn't where you're
*   meant to be*

It's easy
All you need is love
All you need is love
All you need is love, love
Love is all you need
All you need is love (all together now)
All you need is love (everybody)
All you need is love, love
Love is all you need
Love is all you need
(Love is all you need)
Love is all you need
(Love is all you need)
Love is all you need
(Love is all you need)
Love is all you need
(Love is all you need)
Love is all you need
(Love is all you need)
Love is all you need
(Love is all you need)
Love is all you need
(Love is all you need)
Love is all you need
(Love is all you need)
Love is all you need
(Love is all you need)
Love is all you need
(Love is all you need)
Love is all you need
(Love is all you need)
Love is all you need
(Love is all you need)
(Love is all you need)
(Love is all you need)
(Love is all you need)
Yesterday
(Love is all you need)

Oh
Love is all you need
Love is all you need
Oh yeah
Love is all you need
(She loves you, yeah, yeah, yeah)
(She loves you, yeah, yeah, yeah)
(Love is all you need)
(Love is all you need)

Source: LyricFind
Songwriters: John Lennon / Paul Mccartney
All You Need Is Love (Remastered 2009) lyrics ©
Sony/ATV Music Publishing LLC

How do you define love? There are so many different ways to define love. I recently watched a Lifetime Christmas movie. As you might know, these stories can all have the same plot: guy and girl meet randomly and develop a love for each other. In this movie I was watching, there was a line that I thought was intriguing. The mother of a lady who came home to visit told her that love is a choice. You make a choice, and you work with what you've got. This means that if you like somebody, have a conversation with them like two adults who are communicating to see if there is reason to have an LTR or long-term relationship.

Personal Experience with Dating

When I divorced, I was packing and found an old journal I had days before I met my ex-wife and then eventually asked her to marry me. It said, "I think I am giving up on dating. I keep trying to meet and date ladies, and nothing seems to ever work out for me." I know that for me I found myself almost giving up on dating back when I was twenty-four years old. I think it is important for me to share that our mindset can really be affected when we have negative experiences with dating. As a young man between the ages of eighteen and twenty-four, I found myself trying to date, yet I had no one to advise me how to date. I really did not date much at all. Just every once in a while, I would meet or run into a lady I thought I liked. And if I had the guts to ask them out, I had some say yes and most say "No!" I think I would be classified as a nerd back in the late 1990s and early 2000s. I had very low self-esteem, dressed funny, and was expressing myself in many different ways. I got my first ear piercing at nineteen and grew my hair long at twenty. That was the extent of outward expressing by yours truly! I even started drinking coffee at twenty-one when I met a young lady who loved Starbucks! Yes, I can pinpoint that time at twenty-one when I was drinking coffee because I liked a girl. Looking back, it's funny yet also seems like a stupid reason to become addicted to coffee and caffeine. I was so naive as a young adult. I did not know anything about love, dating, how much work it takes in a marriage, and how to manage my own money. I even remember at age eighteen liking a girl and all I knew to do was sit close beside her and hold her hand and listen to her.

People

People come in different shapes and sizes
Different looks, different strokes
Sitting across from many
Shows me how amazing we all are
Some are extravagant
Others small
Some loud
Others soft
In all ways acknowledge him
Who made us all very cool
The Maker of heaven is awesome
Why be so mean?
Why be so anxious?
In the end God's in control
Friendly faces meet sorry faces
Each one in their own world
All people are cool
Let us look upon others for bravery
Just like in Daniel, the little guy won
Why should we be so large?
Does the little man humble us?
Does the large man scare us?
All we know is that God made
His people different for a reason
Reason being…
Find out for yourself
It is different for everyone
God is love and all
We, like sheep, have gone astray

If one is strong and
Another small
Will we ever get along?
Just remember that God
Made us different for
A purpose
To help each other
And be a friend like Jesus!

One-Month Love

Why does most love
Last one month long?
Jesus Christ,
What would Jesus do?
I feel that every time I meet a lady,
The real intimacy only lasts for a month.
I know I didn't lose a friend.
I gained a friend.
Jesus Christ lived,
Knowing that he would die, kinda.
He loved everyone.
He didn't worry about a girlfriend.
He just became friends of his acquaintances.
Jesus would be glad that my friends
Accepted him,
Not worrying
About a long-term relationship.
But…
Why, Lord, do you show me these
Women,
Beautiful as ever,
Loving me ever more than any other?
I know this is all "criticism,"
All for learning,
All for experience,
To lead
To the perfect woman for me,
To the awesome love God is
Saving for me through her,

Just as I will give this love
To her, unconditionally.
Life is hard,
But
Pray hard (1 Thessalonians 5:17).
Women, one of God's greatest loves—
They care for you
As your mother cares for you.
I thank the women in my life for
Loving me
But
Especially for molding me,
Helping me
To become a better person.
I hope I helped them as much.
God, I pray.

Angela

(The most beautiful woman I ever knew)

We met by coincidence
Over the counter of an office
Wanting me to love another
Enjoying the voice of her
Day by day
Hour by hour
Minute by minute
We grew as flowers grow
Friends forever
Loving each other as a woman loves her man
I love her as God loves her
I need her, as her daughter needs her
This love is special
Many activities did we do
Many activities did we enjoy
Many activities we blossomed as lovely friends
Many times we hung out and enjoyed each oth-
      er's presence
Until one day we felt confused
Are we more than friends?
Will there ever be an intimate moment?
I ask, What is your will, oh God?
We will always be friends
Love endures forever
We do love each other
But to the point that
We support each other as close friends
What I want to know is, Why?
Why do I feel empty?

Why do I feel as if I lost my friend?
Why, God? Why me?
Is this all for the best?
Am I learning?
Many questions in my head
Many sins lingering back into my mind
Many times I feel sad
Thinking I might need a woman
Thinking, wishing, wanting
Angela
To become my close friend again
Tell me why I dream about her
Tell me why I feel loved around her
Tell me why she comforts me
If anything, thanks for giving
A friendship,
A love,
Compassion,
And a hand to hold onto in public
I love you, Angela
Prayer is best
Pain means I am loved

(For everyone who has been through unconditional love)

Personal Counseling to Share

As mentioned before, I'll be asking a lot of questions as I gather some background information from you. You never have to answer anything that you don't feel comfortable with. Also, it is very important to me that if at any point you feel like we are not going down the path you want us to be going down or we are not focusing on what you want to focus on, you let me know. We can always readjust as needed. Counseling is a process, one in which I do my best to take cues from you. It's important for you to let me know if you think we are missing something at any point. I always want to be sure your needs are being met as much as possible.

I'd like to ask you some questions now. I apologize if some of these questions you already answered in the initial form you filled out; I just like to clarify things.

What are your goals for counseling? I want to share my co-parenting struggles and get another professional opinion if I need to do anything differently.

Can you tell me a little bit more about yourself? How many people are in your household, and who makes up your household? I was separated one year ago and divorced six months. I live alone. I have my kids over for dinner twice a week and host them every other weekend.

What kind of support system do you have? Are you married or in a relationship? If so, for how long? Do you have family and friends that you are close with? If you have children, what are their genders and ages? I have a couple close friends, have been meeting a number of new friends, and have moments when I feel alone and unsure who to call for help. I am trying to date again. I was married for almost seventeen years. I have two close guy friends and have some new lady friends. I have three kids: girl, fourteen; girl, twelve; boy, ten.

Could you tell me what you see as your strengths and weaknesses? I have a weakness of not thinking for myself. I have strong intuition and strong empathy for others and am a hard worker.

Do you have any special interests and hobbies? What do you do for fun? What do you do to relax? I enjoy watching sports, reading, watching HGTV shows, walking, and exploring. Also, I am trying to write a book. I like to walk as much as I can. I enjoy cooking. Music is the main thing that helps me relax.

How do you handle stress and difficult situations in your life? What do you find helpful, and what have you tried that is not helpful? Deep breathing works best for me, talking with friends as well. Being outdoors is my favorite place to be. I use CBT techniques. I am a thinker.

Could you tell me about your job, if you have one, as well as your work history and educational background? I work for Blue Cross as an appeals reviewer. Then I offer counseling a couple times a week, mainly online. I have been a teacher's aide, counselor, and managed care worker. I have had jobs as a janitor and fast-food place worker. I have degrees from religious schools and a master's degree in counseling.

How are things for you financially? Do you have any financial concerns? I am okay financially for just being divorced. I don't like all the debt I have after my divorce. I wish for a better job just doing counseling. I have not figured how to make that happen with child support and debt and bills.

Do you have any spiritual beliefs; and if so, could you tell me about them and how they fit into your life? I used to be really religious. Now I have bad feelings about organized religion. I call myself spiritual these days. I do believe in God and that he made our world. I just don't put all my eggs in the church basket anymore.

Have you ever been in counseling before? If so, would you mind sharing a little bit about your experience so I know what you focused on, what helped, and what didn't help? Is there any particular style or approach that you feel fits you best or anything you think would be helpful for me to know? I have done counseling numerous times. I recently had a bad experience with a marriage counselor when my ex and I were separated. I felt like she took my ex's side and did not hear my point at all. I need a counselor who will listen to my opinion and at least acknowledge my perspective and that counselor can disagree. I want a counselor to respect me!

Have you ever been given any mental health diagnoses (i.e., ADHD, depression, anxiety)? If so, when were you diagnosed and who diagnosed you (i.e., primary care physician, psychiatrist, therapist)? I have been given the following diagnoses: PTSD, depression. A psychologist gave me the PTSD dx. My PCP gave me the depression dx.

Are you currently taking any psychotropics (medications to manage mental health symptoms)? None.

Do you have any health concerns or chronic conditions? If so, would you mind sharing more about them? Do you take any medications for physical health purposes? I have a hip impingement. I don't take anything currently. It is not that bad.

Do you have any concerns about alcohol or other substance usage? Nope.

Do you ever feel unsafe or threatened in any way in your present living situation? Have you ever experienced any physical, emotional, mental, or sexual abuse in the past? If so, and you are comfortable, would you mind sharing a little bit about your experience and any help you received afterward? No, I experienced trauma in middle school when I was bullied severely, pushed, and spoke down to.

Do you have any time frame in mind regarding how long you would like to be in counseling for, or is that open-ended? Some people remain in counseling for years, while others plan to try it for weeks or months. I just like to ask so I know what your expectations are. If you haven't thought about that, that's okay. I think it's always best to just see how things flow. There is no time limit here! I want to use my five free counseling sessions from my EAP. I am thinking I want to meet every other week.

Lastly, please feel free to ask me any questions you'd like to! I've certainly done my part in getting to know you. Now it is your turn, if you wish!

How long have you been counseling? Include your practicum time in your master's program.

Do you have a religious side to your counseling? I don't want that but am open to it.

Please feel free to take your time responding and/or respond in segments if that is easier for you. I know I've thrown a lot at you. I appreciate you bearing with me, and I hope I haven't overwhelmed you too much!

I can't promise this will be the end of my questioning. As I read through your responses in order to write a meaningful response myself, I may come across something that requires clarification or more information. As always, don't feel you have to answer if you don't want to.

Thank you for your patience through this intake process. I'm looking forward to getting to learn more about you!

Christmas Morning *Feeling surprised* 😵

I want to share one moment this morning that was uncomfortable for me. I went to my ex's house to have Christmas with my kids. When my ex asked if I wanted anything to eat and I said "No, thanks," I could tell that she was mad at me. I did apologize later. I apologized for hurting her feelings. I apologized as a way to make her feel better. I probably didn't have to do that, but I did. I feel like I made a choice that I wasn't hungry and I made a choice to hold that boundary. I think that she thinks she knows what's best for everybody, yet I think it was inappropriate to be mad at me for not wanting to eat all her food she made.

Don't Forget the Past

Today is December 25, 2020. I woke up alone. That is nothing new to my new life. I was getting ready for my day and to go to have Christmas with my kids at my ex-wife's place. I was thinking about nineteen years ago, December 25, 2001. This was the last time I woke up as a single person on Christmas Day. I lived in DeWitt, Iowa. I had two jobs, youth pastor at the United Methodist Church and a teacher's aide at the local school district. I felt surprised that I did not remember what I did on that day. Did I drive back to Central Iowa to have Christmas with my parents and sister and brother-in-law and one nephew with nephew number two on the way a month after Christmas? I really have no recollection of that day nineteen years ago. This is what I wanted to share with the reader: I think it is important to not forget our past holiday memories. It is a perfect example how I lost myself in my marriage. I had this life in Iowa. But after eighteen years of living in Texas, I really seem to forget those years of my life, and I think that is sad. All I know is my past is something that I want to remember now that I am single again. I wish I would have done a better job of writing down these memories or made it a better point to remember my years before being married.

The past is important to remember because it shows what is important to me. I now wish I would have done a better job of holding on to the things that are important to me. I found myself as a married man, laying down what was important to me and choosing to do what was important to my ex-wife. I will say there can be elements of that being okay, yet we all should never lose ourselves just because another person thinks it is more important than what we think is important. If you are in a relationship and you find yourself doing what your partner wants more than your own ideas, I think you should take time and question the current values and ask yourself, "Are these my values or someone else's?"

I called my mom to ask her if she remembered what I did nineteen years ago. She didn't answer, so I had to leave a message asking her. Sometimes when we want a family member to answer and help us remember, they are not available. The lesson to learn is don't rely on others to remember for you. My plan is to do better the rest of my life to remember important memories on important dates. I wonder if I will I lose my ability to remember the older I get. Then I better use this platform in order to write my memories.

Listen, here! If you are saying, "I have a great memory, and I have a great ability to not let others' goals overshadow my own goals!" well, good for you. I have not met many people who have learned to be strong themselves and not lose themselves in a relationship. Well, my parents called me back. They said that back on December 25, 2001, I came home for Christmas because they remembered a picture of me with them and my sister who was expecting her second child. I guess sometimes it helps to ask family to help you remember. They said to me on the phone, "You never missed a Christmas!" It makes me sad that I have missed a lot more Christmases with my family after moving out of state. (I think I am a bit emotional today knowing that I am single and I am not physically close to my family.)

I enjoyed hearing my mom share a story about my sister's memory of my Grandma Overman. She used to carefully unwrap presents in order to save the wrapping paper. She did grow up during the Great Depression. This is rambling on typing, yet there is some lesson to be learned here.

In life, divorce happens. People forget about old family traditions. People are sad during the holidays when they are used to having a family around. People lose themselves in relationships. People are pussies. People make mistakes. People may never say they are sorry for treating you like shit. People may act selfish because that is our world these days. People shut down. People act suicidal. People have panic attacks. People are mean. People will never understand. People care yet might not know how to express it. People hurt other people's feelings. People break brand-new iPhone screens on Christmas morning. People lose the charging port that goes in the wall on Christmas morning. People get very angry when things don't go their way.

Why can't we all just learn to accept failure and learn to be patient and loving with everyone we meet? I know I am not perfect. I have made choices that have pissed people off, and I have made choices that have made people my enemy. Life is challenging. Life hurts. Life also is beautiful and can be enjoyed with the right mindset about things. We can make plans that we think make sense to us. Those plans can get tossed out in an instant, and we need to be flexible about plans changing. I love what a colleague once said in a book I read. My paraphrase: Why can't we all just learn to not let life throw off our day and make the best of what we got? Rather than say "Whatever" and roll our eyes, let's look up in the sky and appreciate the fact we are alive and able to breathe fresh air and have our eyesight to view beautiful landscapes and sunrises and sunsets and mountains and lakes and rivers and nature in general. Man, writing a book can be hard. I have been writing my random thoughts down on this Google Drive for eleven months, and I am only one-seventh of the way done. I do have future thinking that it will become a book that at least a few people appreciate and that helps at least one couple to really reevaluate their relationship. I think it is time to stop for today.

One-Year Anniversary of Being Separated

I have had too many sleepless nights, too many fights, and too many moments of drama with my ex-wife.

When I don't have my kids, I feel lonely. I have plenty of activities to occupy my time, yet there is still a void inside me, and I have yet to figure out what goes in that void.

My best friend said, "Enjoy life and be happy."

My best friend reminded me my ex-wife would not let me have female friends. He reminded me of a time that I followed *The Amazing Race* and messaged a female race participant on Twitter and how my ex got mad at me for messaging this other female.

I find myself having plenty of activities to keep me busy. My best friend seems to think I am not doing the activities that make me happy.

It is a new year. Today is January 2, 2021. I guess this would be the best time to try some new, never-considered activities. This shy guy says it may be hard. We have to step out of our comfort zones. I know we do!

It dawned on me that I am like Mike Brady. I have three young children as a single dad.

Dreams

Today is January 3, 2021.

I want to share a dream I had right before I woke up this morning.

It was nighttime.

I was at an unknown location.

I came up to this object sitting on a rock ledge off a building.

I picked up the object, and it looked like a very old object.

There was an older man, like a collector.

He said to me, "Open it."

Beside the object were different tools for me to use to open the object.

I picked up the object and studied where it looked like a key was to be inserted.

I tried a number of keys. Nothing was working.

The old man said, "Look inside the small red box." This appeared to be something that came off the object.

I looked inside this small red box, and there was a very small key.

I placed this very small key inside the smallest hole I found on this object.

The object opened up and began expanding and even began making a material like paper that started coming out.

Then I woke up.

What does this mean?

Carl Jung was a Swiss psychiatrist and psychoanalyst. He believed dreams were the unconscious trying to become conscious.

I think my dream means that I have been looking all over for the key to my happiness, when all along it has always been inside of me. I now know that I need to trust my intuition more and find the key to my happiness. I think the old man represents how I have a pattern of asking others for help when I have the ability to make decisions all by myself.

Can Astrology Really Help Us Understand Ourselves Better?

I have begun to study astrology lately. It fascinates me how doing a birth chart and then studying what each element of the birth chart means can explain my personality and more. I am a novice, yet this is very interesting to me, especially since I was into organized religion for so many years.

Moving to Dallas, Texas

August 20, 2002, Tuesday

I drove from Colo, Iowa, to Oklahoma. I thought too much about worries down there. The car had to move slow. I was very tired and relaxed in Joan and Steve's pool. I am glad these guys are only a few hours away.

August 21, 2002, Wednesday

I drove to Dallas. I felt rushed like I didn't have time to organize stuff. I looked at apartments after being almost cut off. I kinda felt scared not knowing what was going to happen. I met up with Bryan. The car almost overheated. After apartment hunting, I was very tired. I had supper with Pete, hung out in the evening with his roommates, and sorta found two apartments. God, which one do I take? I showered.

Honestly, I am unhappy and confused. I am wondering why I am here yet don't feel very comfortable. God, give me clarity. God, I pray for an apartment and for a new clarity and safety for my stuff outside. I am having second thoughts about being here, yet the people I've met are cool. God, I know you've blessed me a lot, yet I am confused about everything. I can grow from this. It's hard. I feel like I am a vapor just flying thru the days. Mom and Dad and people know I am here, and I think that you've brought some neat people to talk with me, God. Thanks. Just encourage me. Help me. Give me understanding. I am in Dallas, Texas. *Wow!*

Make Sure You Take a Job for the Right Reasons, Not for the Wrong Ones!

Today is January 4, 2021. I have this day job that is managing cases for a health insurance company. Today I sit here, and I think this is not the right job for me. I took the job because my ex-wife suggested it to make more money for the family. It just brings up an important lesson. Don't take a job because a spouse wants you to. I think we all need to take a job because we want to and not to please other people. I don't hate my job. I am just learning so much more about myself, and I know there could be a better job that highlights all my skills. I just wanted to write how careers are sometimes influenced by people and sometimes those influences are not the best for us. We know better than anyone! LinkedIn and Indeed are two very helpful sites/apps that allow us to look into other options.

The Start of 2021

January 15, 2021

I just wanted to say that I feel unsupported. I feel like my kids don't want to spend time with me. I feel rejected by my children. It hurts when my kids say to me they don't want to spend time with me on my birthday weekend.

January 16, 2021

I live three miles from the house I had with my ex-wife; it is too close. I want to live farther when I move into a house.

I live six miles from Cottonwood Creek Church, which hosts the club volleyball team where my two girls play volleyball.

My son is the only child who likes spending time with me. We had a great evening of watching *The Goldbergs* and NBA basketball while we ate food together.

January 18, 2021

I am currently in an airplane flying from Charlotte, North Carolina, to Myrtle Beach, South Carolina. I didn't realize when I put my iPhone in airplane mode that I couldn't listen to my music playlists I made on Amazon Music. So I thought I'd share some thoughts with you all.

Everyone traveling from Dallas/Fort Worth Airport to Charlotte made me realize we all need connection! We are all wearing masks. No one is talking. People are either sleeping or on a device or *reading*. At least that's what I ended up doing!

On this flight, there are fewer people traveling, and I get a whole row to myself! The other flight was packed, so this is a positive thing for sure.

This is my first time traveling on a plane without a spouse to text and update on how things are going. I do have a couple friends who have messaged me!

I do enjoy traveling alone!

So one thing I was doing on my last flight was looking through the pictures since separated from my ex-wife. I saw memories, good and bad. I saw friends I've kept and those I've chosen to leave. 2020 was hard. I almost was having second thoughts about those I've left. With it being 2021, I have so much. I was talking with a friend this last weekend. We discussed how people thrive. His suggestion was that people who feel they are progressing themselves are happiest.

One of the books that I read when I was in my early twenties was *Finding the Love of Your Life* by Neil Clark Warren. This is a book that really takes me back. I remember reading it and thinking how it had the key to finding the right wife. This book is in the religious genre. I get angry thinking about how religious literature was influenced by thinking back then. At the time I was a supporter of religious literature. That desire has decreased over the years for me.

I am learning how to be happy alone!

I think those of us who are codependent need to learn how to entertain ourselves alone. Of course we all need social interaction. I just think it is important to learn how to entertain ourselves. Making a list of the things that you enjoy doing alone would be a great place to start.

My list of free activities would be walking, reading a book, and writing. My list of activities that cost money would be eating and drinking good food and drinks, driving around, traveling, visiting museums, and gardening.

January 29, 2021

I picked up my three kids tonight at their mom's house. I took my oldest to her volleyball practice, then drove to my apartment, and made food for me and my other two kids. Then around 9:15 p.m., I had to leave my two kids at my place and go pick up my oldest from her volleyball practice. I drove her to her mom's house because she said she needed to sleep in her bed to get good sleep for her volleyball tournament in the morning. When I dropped her off, she said, "Mom's friend's here." I automatically felt jealous. I did not speak anything to my daughter. I just wished her a good night. Driving home to my place, I could not help but think how much I struggled with feelings of jealousy.

Today during my work lunch hour, I had my own counseling session. My counselor identified that I had a thinking error called "all or nothing thinking." This all or nothing thinking error means that numerous times I can think this way. During my counseling, I shared how I recently had contacted a male friend who I said I did not want to be friends with anymore, to see if we could reconcile the friendship. This person wrote back and said, "I do not want to be close friends, but I will get drinks and shoot the shit with you" (my paraphrase). My counselor stated, "It seems like you put friendships into an all or nothing category." It really made me think that I needed to reevaluate my friendships. The counselor also commented on finding happiness alone. I was codependent on my ex-wife. That was not healthy. I needed to be able to see my ex-wife being social with her friends and not get jealous.

I have not found my physical location where I feel at home. I grew up in Iowa and lived in Iowa for twenty-four years. I moved to Texas. As of August of 2020, I have lived here in Texas for eighteen years. I want to travel to every state in the United States and see which state I feel at home in. I also know I need to learn how to be happy in the present. It is so important to be happy where you are. I know from personal experience it is hard to find happiness when one feels like their life has been directed by others and not themselves. Yet we all make choices and find ourselves making choices that at the time seem like good ideas. When I married, I really did want to marry my ex-wife. Yet overtime the relationship just became unhealthy in so many ways. It is still hard for me to not get jealous when others seem to have friends to hang out with while I do not seem to have those friends right now. The nights are so hard for me. For some reason, darkness can make me sad. I have learned about seasonal affective disorder, but I wonder if there is a name for feeling sad at night. I just looked on my friend Google to see what it says. What makes sense to me is rumination. I struggle with rumination a lot! I am an overthinker. I know it is hard. Learn from me. When you are in your early twenties, figure out a way to be happy alone. Figure out a way to feed your soul. Find a way to learn to not be jealous of others. That to me is a sign of codependency. Codependency is not healthy. Learn to find happiness inside of yourself. Do not look to others to satisfy your personal needs.

February 5, 2021

The time was 6:00 p.m. I arrived at my kids' house. My oldest daughter, Chloe, came out to meet me. She appeared upset with me. She opened my vehicle door and said, "Hi!" I responded by saying hello.

She said to me, "Why do I have to stay over at your place? I do not want to stay over at your place."

I responded by saying, "The three of us agreed to this last weekend, Mom, you, and me."

She said, "Well, if I did, I have changed my mind."

I began to raise my voice and stated to her, "You are a brat who thinks you get your way. I disagree with you."

She then left the car and went back into their house.

My oldest daughter then called me asking if I could go take her to Tokyo Joe's to get food. I said no because I was planning on making spaghetti tonight for the kids and me. I hung up the phone.

Doing Taxes after a Divorce

I found a new tax professional for me. I had a free consultation over Zoom on Friday, February 12, 2021. I explained that my ex-wife had always done our taxes for us when we were married. I found myself learning a lot. I was told to send her my divorce decree to help determine a child tax credit. I also learned that I need to figure out mortgage interest on the house my ex-wife and I had for the first six months of the year 2020. Then she asked me if I paid child support. I explained how my ex-wife had not filled out the paper yet. I had sent her the paper recently. My ex-wife would give me two reasons she hadn't done it yet. She said she was busy and she did not feel right having money taken out of my paycheck by the state when I could just Zelle her the money every two weeks. I learned that the Office of the Attorney General of Texas would send a letter for tax purposes to report how much money was spent on child support. Since I told my tax person that my ex-wife had not filled out the paper and submitted it, I was told to give her my Excel spreadsheet of the money I gave to her.

Evaluate Boundaries and Love Languages

I am mad about how anytime my ex-wife texts me, it is to ask for something. I know that it is hard since I was a husband who was a helper for so many years. Saying the word "no" to my ex-wife is a challenge to me. I think her highest love language is acts of service. She appreciates it when others do things for her so she can relax. I want to speak to the people reading this book. If you find a partner who you think reaches out to you to just check on you, that should be evaluated regarding their motivation. Are they motivated to really care about you? Or do they have a hidden agenda? I once learned a lesson of "adding value" to a person's life. Ask yourself, How can I add value to someone else's life? As you get to know someone, you learn about their love language. You learn how they best receive love. Go to this website: https://www.5lovelanguages.com/.

This website has a lot of resources. Take the quiz to find out what your love language is. Ask your partner to take the quiz to determine their love language. Talk about the results together. Have each person give specific examples of their top two love languages so the other person is able to learn exactly how to show that person love the best way possible. I know what my ex-wife's love languages are because we talked about it when we got married. I do think the love languages do change overtime. I know mine did. I recently took the test. My results as of 2021 are physical touch at 33 percent, quality time at 30 percent, words of affirmation at 27 percent, acts of service at 10 percent, and receiving gifts at 0 percent.

Light Bulb Moment

When a child asks you to share your side of the divorce, what do you say?

I asked counseling colleagues and personal friends to see what they would suggest.

Then I chose to come up with an idea on my own to be proud of what I chose to say.

Positive traits? Nope!

Negative traits? See below.

- Narcissistic
- Selfish
- Controlling
- Lacks empathy
- Lacks sharing the responsibility
- Overtime, not happy with parenting choices made together

We all make choices, and we have to live with them.

Do you tell your kids the truth if they ask?

I said…

I felt like she was more occupied with work and her grandmother who lived with us and less interested in me. I didn't do a good job of communicating my needs. I found myself less interested in her. I also didn't like how she asked me to always run errands, and that seemed controlling or being bossy. I got tired of being controlled or her being bossy.

I realized in March 2020 that the relationship was not healthy. I realized I would be happier alone.

I am happy to do what I want to do!

The lesson learned is I lost myself in my marriage and I'm not letting that happen to me anymore because I am my own person and I deserve to be loved as myself!

Can I love again?

I was recently reminded of this song from 1990:

Love of a Lifetime
Firehouse

I guess the time was right for us to say
We'd take our time and live our lives together day
    by day
We'll make a wish and send it on a prayer
We know our dreams can all come true with love
    that we can share
With you I never wonder
Will you be there for me?
With you I never wonder
You're the right one for me
I finally found the love of a lifetime
A love to last my whole life through
I finally found the love of a lifetime
Forever in my heart
I finally found the love of a lifetime
With every kiss, our love is like brand-new
And every star up in the sky was made for me
    and you
Still we both know that the road is long
We know that we will be together
Because our love is strong
I finally found the love of a lifetime
A love to last my whole life through
I finally found the love of a lifetime
Forever in my heart
I finally found the love of a lifetime

I finally found the love of a lifetime
A love to last my whole life through
I finally found the love of a lifetime
Forever in my heart
I finally found the love of a lifetime
Love of a lifetime (I finally found the love of a
    lifetime)
I finally found a love (I finally found the love of
    a lifetime)
Ooh, forever in my heart
I finally found the love of a lifetime
Ooh, ooh

The End?

It was March 30, 2021, four o'clock in the morning.

I had a very vivid dream, and I think it means I am finally over my previous marriage.

My ex-wife and I were in the driveway of the house we had together.

She showed me a grave.

She said, "I wanted you to not be alone."

She also showed me a grave to the right of the driveway.

I could not read what the grave said on the right of the driveway.

I just remember standing there with her and her showing me this grave.

This grave was elaborate.

When I woke up at four o'clock in the morning, I said, "Wow, that was a very interesting dream."

I think the dream means my ex-wife wants me to move on and be okay with the relationship ending.

This is a good moment in time as I write this on March 30, 2021, at 10:03 a.m.

I am ready to put the previous marriage to death. It is so important to ask what these dreams mean. Dreams are the unconscious showing us that we are processing life, and that is a good thing.

What to do When an Old Friend Whom You Said Goodbye to Contacts You?

On Thursday, March 11, 2021, at 3:23 p.m., I received a text from an old friend with whom last fall I said I did not want to be friends with. Then in January I was on vacation and reached out saying that I was wrong to end the friendship. When I reached out in January, he only said, "We can be whiskey club friends only." So when I received this text message in March, I was surprised. He was on a work trip, and he knew I liked a whiskey made in Missouri, so he asked me if I wanted a bottle. I said, "Yes, sir, thank you." He said he would be back in town the first week of April. As I write this, it is Friday, April 2, 2021. He texted that he was close and wanted to drop the bottle off at my apartment. Is he trying to rekindle some form of relationship? I thanked him for the bottle. We caught up a bit and then said goodbye after discussing recent whiskey pours he recently had. Relationships are confusing sometimes. Remember, every relationship is a choice. Ask yourself this question for everyone you meet: Do I want to be friends with this person? When I was younger, I thought I had to be friends with everyone. Thanks, Dad! My dad was a people pleaser, and the only thing I disagree with is that we have to be friends with everyone. I think I am learning that some friends come and go and come back. Ultimately it is a choice to be friends with anyone. Make sure you are choosing healthy friends and also choosing acquaintances that you do not want to be close friends.

Lady A Song about a Breakup (Can You Relate? I Did!)

What If I Never Get Over You

It's supposed to hurt, it's a broken heart
But the moving on is the hardest part
It comes in waves, the letting go
But the memory fades, everybody knows, every-
body knows

What if I'm trying, but then I close my eyes and
then I'm right back
Lost in that last goodbye, what if time doesn't do
what it's supposed to do?
What if I never get over you?

Maybe months go by, maybe years from now
And I meet someone and it's working out
Every now and then, he can see right through
'Cause when I look at him, yeah, all I see is you

What if I'm trying, but then I close my eyes and
then I'm right back
Lost in that last goodbye, what if time doesn't do
what it's supposed to do?
What if I never get over you?

Ooh yeah
What if I never get over?

What if I never get closure?
What if I never get back all the wasted words I
    told you?
What if it never gets better?
What if this lasts forever and ever and ever, I'm
    tryin'

But then I close my eyes and then I'm right back
Lost in that last goodbye, what if time doesn't do
    what it's supposed to do?
What if I never get over you?

What if I gave you everything I got
What if your love was my one and only shot
What if I end up with nothing to compare it to
What if I never get over—
What if I never get over—
What if I never get over you?

What if I never get over you?
What if I never get it over you?

Coping Skills That Worked for Me!

1. Music
2. Exercise: walking, sit-ups, weights, running
3. Calling and/or texting friends and close family
4. Watching sports or new television shows or old movies I never watched
5. Dancing alone in my apartment
6. Cooking and baking
7. Singing
8. Playing video games on my new PlayStation 4
9. Spending time with my kids
10. Taking vacations by myself
11. Crying
12. Yelling
13. Playing guitar
14. Reading books
15. Buying and taking care of a plant
16. Doing puzzles with my son
17. Doing Legos with my son
18. Teaching my oldest to drive in my new vehicle
19. Going shopping with my daughters
20. Going to a park with my kids
21. Playing basketball with my son
22. Writing a book
23. Cleaning
24. Learning how to manage money better
25. Grocery shopping
26. Volunteering with my daughters' volleyball team during games
27. Chair dancing

28. Meditating on a local meetup group
29. Being an uber-"daddy" for my kids
30. Driving in my new vehicle and visiting a friend
31. Watching old DVDs of my favorite movies

Learn How to Be in Control

October 5, 2021

Today, I woke up late. I'm glad I work from home. I was talking with a new friend, T. I wanted to share something I learned from the conversation: *don't forget myself anymore*! It hit me this morning that I was forgetting my own needs in my marriage. Not a good way to live. Learn from me. It sucked, and it also sucks having to relearn how to practice self-care skills. We all need to be focusing on self-care. I had lost myself. The advice from my new friend really hit me today. I will always have drama in my life. Post-divorce drama sucks, yet it is just a part of my life, and I need to take care of me and not let others' stress get me down.

You know, I also need to share about how I was reading on social media and one person posted how it is important to realize how everyone we meet does not have to be in our life forever. Sometimes people enter our life to shed light on something, to challenge us, or even to piss us off. But ultimately the reason does not matter. What matters is the ability to learn from it and not make the same mistake next time.

Lessons learned from selling life insurance: In life you will hear no a lot, but eventually you will hear a yes, and that can be something to be grateful for. Enemies are part of our world. It is okay to have enemies. Just decide to agree to disagree and move on. Learning to accept that we will have people who we do not get along with will help us learn about those people that we will accept into our lives and become close friends with.

Online dating, October 2021

I have decided to only utilize one app, Bumble. It is the one app that I seem to meet the best and healthiest people. I am selling life insurance and learning how being a salesman is a numbers game. The same numbers game applies to dating—a lesson I really never understood until I became a salesman. So the lesson learned here is sometimes it takes a certain job or activity to teach us how another activity can make more sense in how to date with a purpose.

Intuition?

October 7, 2021

My "Pacific time zone" friend finally made me see something very important today.

She asked me, "What are three things you like about yourself?"

One is that I have good intuition.

So it just dawned on me that at the end of my marriage, I allowed myself to not trust my intuition. Instead, I became a follower of what others suggested I should do. OMG. Why did it take this long to finally figure this out?

Road trip, November 2021

I had a purpose to find some happiness the four days I was on my road trip to Louisiana and the Mississippi Gulf Coast.

I evaluated my life.

I wrote the following:

> Dear kids,
>
> It is Tuesday night. I have had some insights and want to share with you. Happiness for me is when I can do activities without others making me—in other words, have my own business. I don't do well when others press me to work. I

think I don't have the right job to help with my happiness.

I feel like I am happy about my personal life. I know how to take care of myself and entertain myself.

I am disappointed with my current financial situation, which is based on poor financial decisions in my past.

It is now Wednesday, and today I plan to think about *Can I be happy with a job I don't enjoy and with financial concerns?* In other words, *Can I be happy in my current situation?*

Thursday, the lesson learned is to never people-please. Always do what you want, and don't let others persuade you to do anything you don't want to do.

I did a lot of thinking about relationships. I am not ready to have any type of a girlfriend. I do want to continue to meet women and become friends only. I keep wanting a girlfriend, yet I continue to not feel ready.

In conclusion, I appear to continue to search for happiness in the wrong places—women, perfectionism perspective about work, people-pleasing behaviors that I continue to work on, and so on. Basically, I overthink everything, and it will take effort to not worry about things like I used to. I need everyone I know to understand something. I have a big heart that wants to love and show empathy. Sorry if I have played with your heart. I will always be a friend to everyone, and I need to continue to work on myself before I can have any relationship like dating.

One more thing about personal time: I need to do a better job of scheduling me time and stop saying yes to others. I hope this makes sense. Personal time needs to be more me than others.

Social Media Posts That I Choose to Share about My Journey

May 28, 2020, at 5:15 p.m. I wrote my first Facebook post on a group that has been amazing support during my post-divorce life. I am keeping the name private because it needs to stay that way. I just want to share how there are great groups out there for support. As I write this, it is January 4, 2022. And I am grateful for this group over the last year and a half.

July 27, 2020, at 10:05 p.m. I posted, "Score one for liquor and poor judgement" (Sheldon from *The Big Bang Theory*).
I was watching season 1, episode 3, and was laughing my ass off! I think liquor plus poor judgement equals sinning!

November 16, 2020, at 5:18 p.m. I posted, "Is it normal to see a pattern of certain work situations and people in your personal life piss you off? Does anyone else have an overthinking problem out there?"

August 6, 2021, at 6:34 p.m. I posted, "Divorce shit hurts…"
I'm learning that I can't make my oldest stay the night. It has taken me a year to realize that some things are out of my control.
Her mom doesn't help the situation either.
Making the best of what I got!
Support is so important when divorcing. Make sure you find your best group to support you through everything.

Intuition

I have always had great intuition.

I wrote myself a sticky note and placed it on my dresser in my bedroom to remind me to listen to my intuition. I just want to share how we all need to trust our intuition. I recently was watching TikTok and saw a post from "Rocky" (Sylvester Stallone) who said we are all born with common sense and all have the ability to thrive in our world. I just loved hearing that message from him! We all need to find strength within ourselves when we go through a life change!

I got a pet!

On December 26, 2021, I went to DAWG in Denison, Texas, and adopted my new pet—a now five-month-old short-haired black cat. My kids named her Bella, and I love the name. I am a cat dad now. She has definitely helped me have company while I live and work in my apartment alone. The kids love her as well.

TikTok

I have definitely enjoyed posting videos on TikTok. So much of living life is finding ways to entertain yourself. I wish I had learned that lesson earlier, but I am grateful I am learning it now! I can find a way to become happy alone, and that is amazing to me! I hope everyone reading this book can understand I am wishing you all can figure this out "sooner than later."

I began writing this book in February 2020. Nearly two years later, I am still writing this book. Will I finish this book? Will I make time to do it in my busy schedule?

I am still single. Will I meet someone to date? My ex-wife has chosen a significant other, and I am still single. Do we all find a significant other, or do some of us just stay single for a while? I have met friends who say I am not dating and purposely staying single. I meet others who are very quick to jump into a relationship. There are even those people who just want to be friends with benefits. All I can say is, trust your intuition and make sure whatever life throws at you, you are happy in the end!

The end to me means happiness, contentment, gratefulness, flexibility, and forgiveness.

I called my parents on January 2, 2022, and spoke to them openly about my struggles post divorce. It was a challenge to share with them, yet I chose to, and it was helpful to me in the end. They suggested to visit a church again. They knew I had not been going to church for a couple years due to negative feelings about church post divorce. I do love this song by TobyMac. It is called "Forgiveness":

> [Intro: TobyMac]
> 'Cause we all make mistakes sometimes
> And we all step across that line
> But nothing's sweeter than the day we find, we
>   find…
>
> [Verse 1: TobyMac]
> It's hangin' over him like the clouds of Seattle
> And rainin' on his swag, fallin' deeper in the saddle
> It's written on his face, he don't have to speak a
>   sound
> Somebody call the Five-0, we got a man down
>
> [Pre-Chorus: TobyMac]
> Now you can go and play it like you're all rock
>   and roll
> But guilt does a job on each and every man's soul
> And when your head hits the pillow at the nightfall
> You can bet your life that it's gonna be a fight, y'all
> [Chorus: TobyMac]
> 'Cause we all make mistakes sometimes

And we've all stepped across that line
But nothing's sweeter than the day we find
Forgiveness (forgiveness), forgiveness (forgiveness)
And we all stumble and we fall
Bridges burn in the heat of it all
But nothing's sweeter than the day
Sweeter than the day we call
[Post-Chorus: TobyMac, *Lecrae*]
Out for forgiveness (Forgiveness)
We all need, we all need
We all need forgiveness (Forgiveness)
We all need, we all need
Mr. Lecrae *(uh)*

[Verse 2: Lecrae]
My momma told me what I would be in for
If I kept all this anger inside of me pent up
My heart been broken, my wounds been open
And I don't know if I can hear "I'm sorry" being
    spoken
But those forgiven much should be quicker to
    give it
And God forgave me for it all, Jesus bled forgiveness
So when the stones fly, and they aimed at you
Just say, "Forgive 'em, Father, they know not
    what they do"
[Pre-Chorus: TobyMac, *TobyMac & Nirva Ready*]
You can go and play it like you're all rock and roll
But guilt does a job on each and every man's soul
And when your head hits the pillow at the nightfall
You can bet your life that it's gonna be a fight, y'all
[Chorus: TobyMac]
Cause we all make mistakes sometimes
And we've all stepped across that line
But nothing's sweeter than the day we find
Forgiveness (forgiveness), forgiveness (forgiveness)

And we all stumble and we fall
Bridges burn in the heat of it all
But nothing's sweeter than the day
Sweeter than the day we call
[Post-Chorus: TobyMac, *Lecrae*]
Out for forgiveness *(Woo, uh, you know we need that)*
(That, that, you know we need that) Forgiveness
(That, that, you know we need that)
(That, yeah, let's talk to 'em)

[Bridge: TobyMac]
No matter how lost you are
You're not that far, you're not too far (Forgiveness)
No matter how hurt you are
You're not that far, you're not too far (Forgiveness)
No matter how wrong you are
You're not that far, you're not too far (Forgiveness)
No matter who you are
You're not that far, you're not too far
From forgiveness (Oh, oh)
Ask for forgiveness (Oh, oh, oh)

[Chorus: TobyMac]
Cause we all make mistakes sometimes (Sometimes)
And we've all stepped across that line (Crossed that line)
But nothing's sweeter than the day we find
Forgiveness (forgiveness), forgiveness (forgiveness)
And we all stumble and we fall
Bridges burn in the heat of it all
But nothing's sweeter than the day
Sweeter than the day we call
[Post-Chorus: TobyMac]
Out for forgiveness (Forgiveness)
We all need, we all need

We all need forgiveness (Forgiveness)
We all need, we all need

[Outro: TobyMac, *Lecrae*]
No matter how lost you are
We all need *(Forgiveness)*
No matter how hurt you are *(Uh-huh)*
We all need *(Forgiveness, forgiveness)* (Forgiveness)
And no matter how wrong you are
You're not that far, you're not too far *(Forgiveness)*
No matter who you are *(Woo)*
You're not too far, you're not too far

We all need (You know we, you know we)
Forgiveness, forgiveness (We all need) (Forgiveness)
We all need (Uh, yeah, you know we, you know)
Forgiveness, forgiveness (We all need) (We all need)
We all need (We do)
Forgiveness, forgiveness (You know we, you know
    we, we all need) (Forgiveness)
We all need (Come on)
Forgiveness, forgiveness (Yeah)

I believe in a higher power in our world. I think forgiveness is important to finding healing in a divorce.

I forgive myself first for all the mistakes I made in my first and only marriage.

I forgive my ex-wife.

I forgive others who hurt me in the past.

Forgiveness is difficult, yet it can bring healing in the end!

The end is up to you!

What does the end look like for you?

What is the next plan?

The end is up to you!

About the Author

Jason Andrew has over fifteen years of counseling experience, and a multitude of clients have praised his work as a counselor. From working in community mental health settings to private practice, he has developed skills to help people of all ages and with numerous concerns. Writing a book was his next goal to further his career as a counselor. He is a divorced father with three kids and currently resides in Van Alstyne, Texas.

looking at the stained
  towel from dying your
    hair (a fail) makes me
      miss you

CPSIA information can be obtained
at www.ICGtesting.com
Printed in the USA
BVHW050157171022
649604BV00005B/107